I CAN FEEL THE
RHYTHM
BY GREG GILPIN

8 Rhythm-Teaching Chorals Using Vocal Speech

Shawnee Press, Inc. &

1221 17th Avenue South • Nashville, TN 37212

Visit Shawnee Press Online at www.shawneepress.com

FOREWORD

From my experience, musicians who sing but do not play an instrument are not very good at reading rhythms. I decided the best way to help the music educator teach rhythms and for the singer to learn rhythms is to take the "notes" out of the song. No singing, just speaking in a rhythmic way.

This collection contains eight chorals that are fun to learn, interesting to teach and entertaining for both performer and listener. You'll find something for the holidays and patriotic celebrations, as well as a piece that teaches how to sing softly and to "sing" musical rests. Your singers will learn how rhythms look, sound and feel and will be able to add their own musicianship skills throughout each piece.

I hesitated in adding dynamics, but it gives you an idea of my intention. Please choose to change these dynamics and create them the way you or your students would like them to be. It's very obvious when your students begin reading, that the pitch, tone and dynamic of their voice are so much more important now. Rhythmic as well as lyrical interpretation through dynamics is now a must! No hiding behind the melodies and harmonies.

The pieces have a swing feel. It seemed this rhythmic feel fit my ideas the best. I tried to keep the songs diverse enough for you to use throughout the year and the lyrics inspirational and educational. Get those pencils out, study these rhythms, interpret the styles and lyrics and enjoy!

I can feel the rhythm! Can you? Continued success!

Greg Gilpin

DO YOU FEEL THE RHYTHM?

for 4-part speech choir, any combination, and drums*

by
GREG GILPIN (ASCAP)

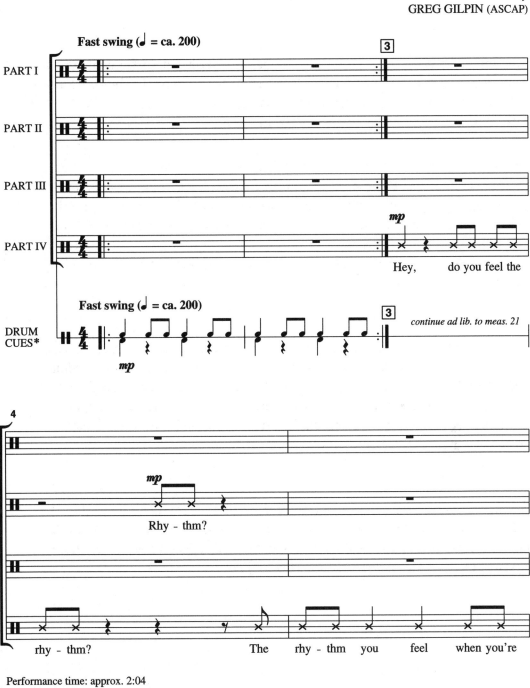

Performance time: approx. 2:04
Drum part is on page 84.
* Available: StudioTrax CD (CD0349)

A0112

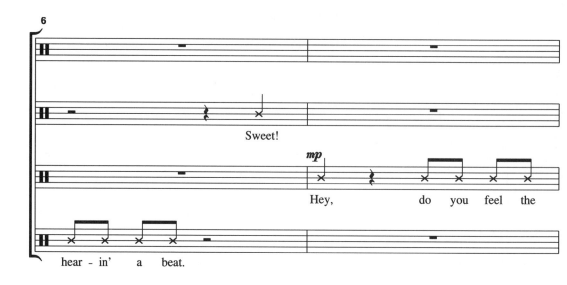

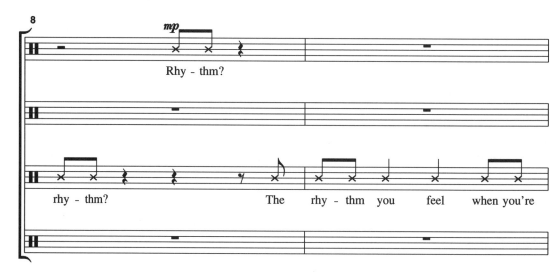

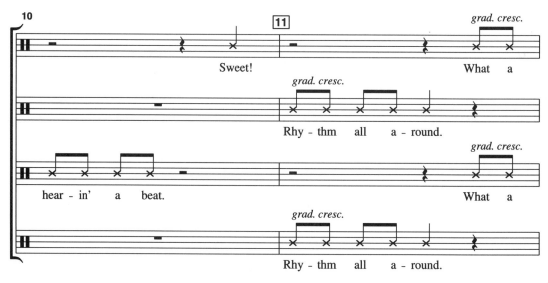

8

9

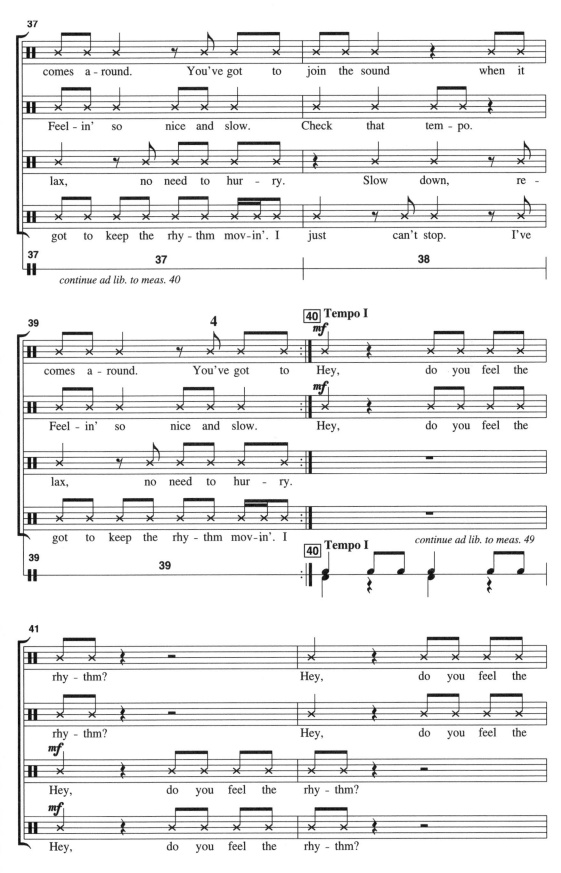

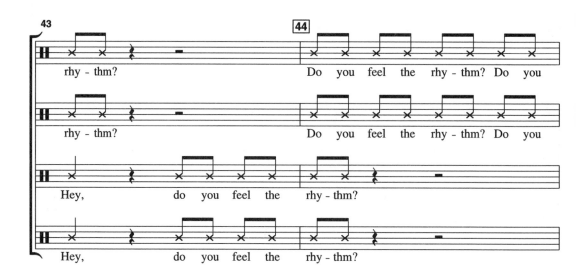

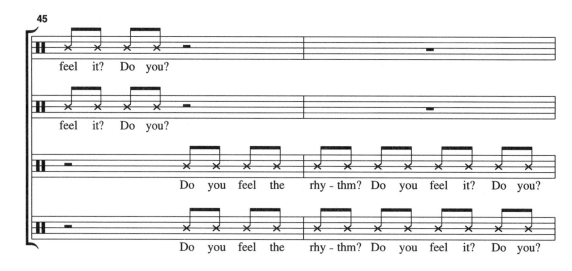

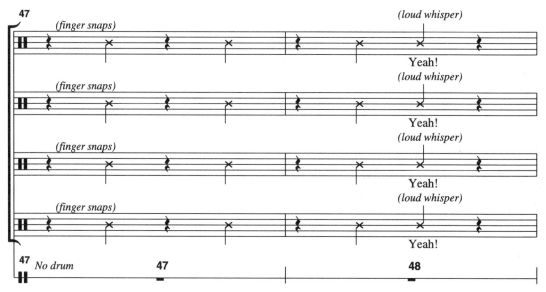

55

Sweet!

rhy - thm you feel when you're hear - in' a beat.

57

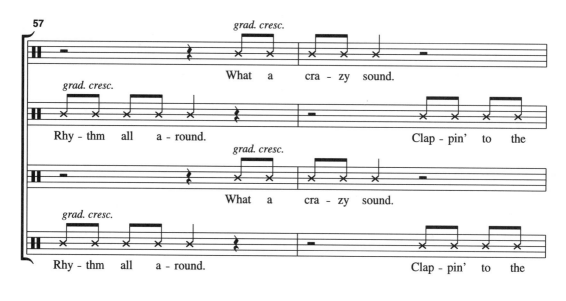

grad. cresc.

What a cra - zy sound.

grad. cresc.

Rhy - thm all a - round.

Clap - pin' to the

grad. cresc.

What a cra - zy sound.

grad. cresc.

Rhy - thm all a - round.

Clap - pin' to the

59

60

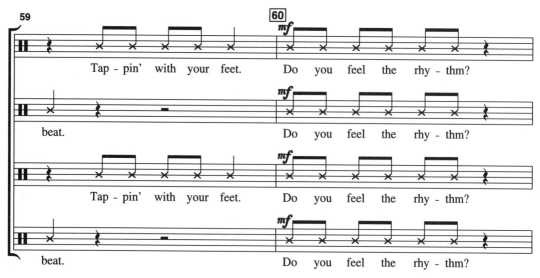

mf

Tap - pin' with your feet. Do you feel the rhy - thm?

mf

beat. Do you feel the rhy - thm?

mf

Tap - pin' with your feet. Do you feel the rhy - thm?

mf

beat. Do you feel the rhy - thm?

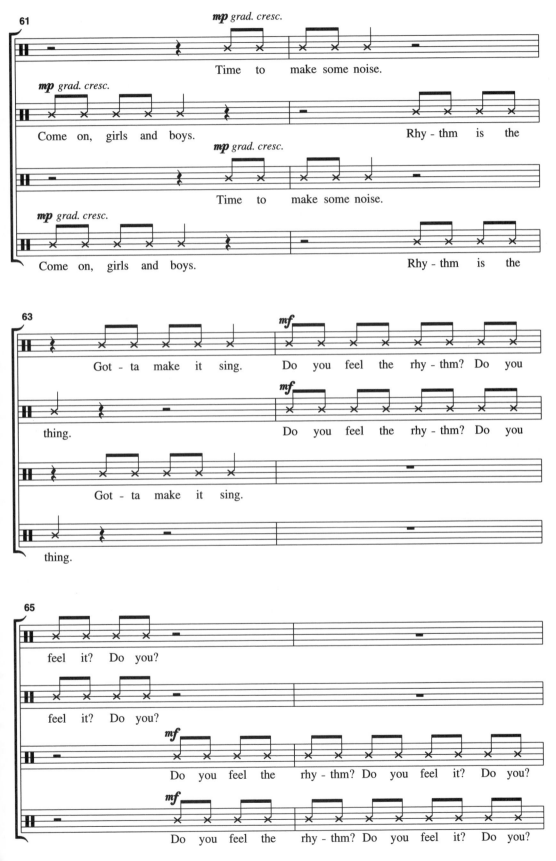

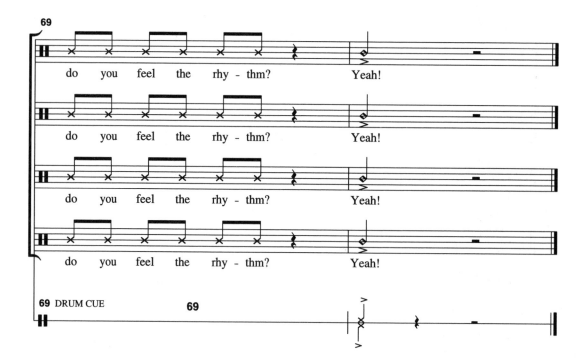

ROCK, RHYTHM AND ROLL

for 4-part speech choir, any combination, and drums*

by
GREG GILPIN (ASCAP)

Performance Time: approx. 1:58
Drum part is on page 85.
*Available: Studio Trax CD (CD0349).

GA0112

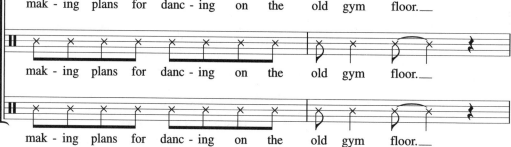

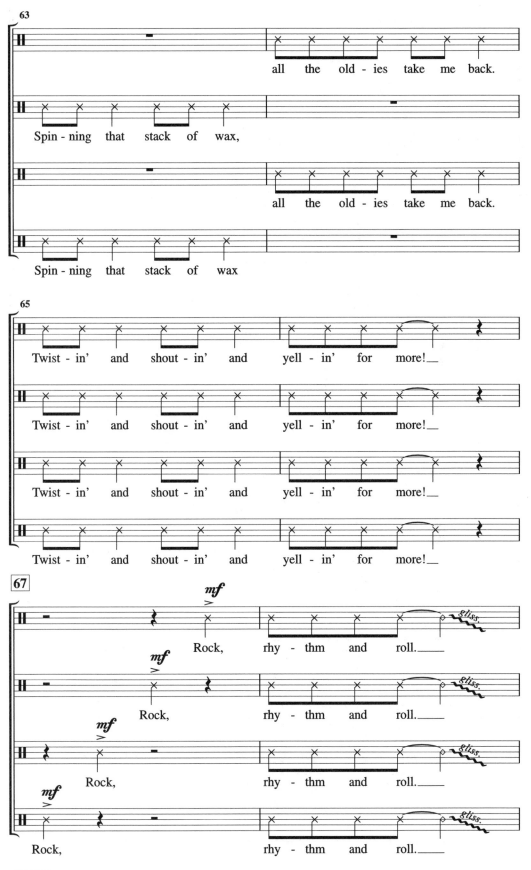

YANKEE DOODLE RHYTHM

for 4-part speech choir, any combination, and drums*

by
GREG GILPIN (ASCAP)

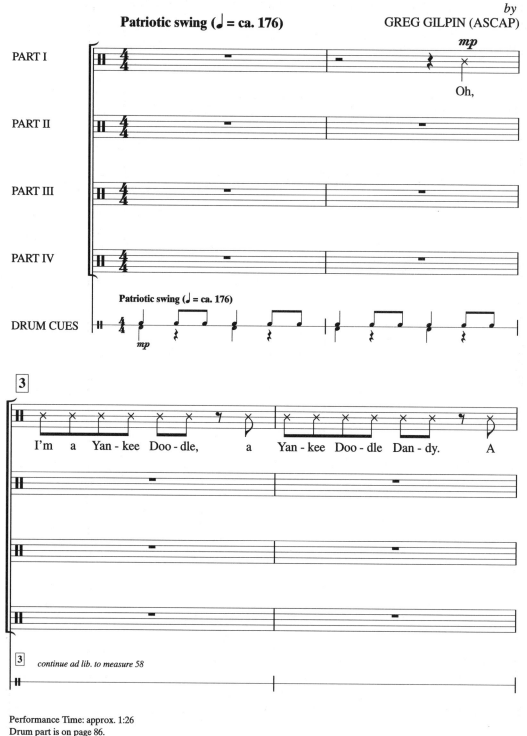

Performance Time: approx. 1:26
Drum part is on page 86.
*Available: Studio Trax CD (CD0349).

GA0112

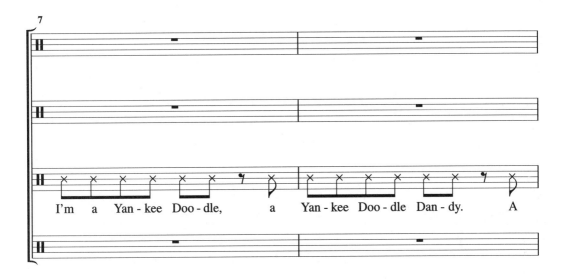

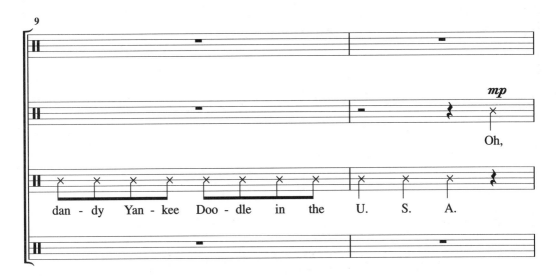

11

13

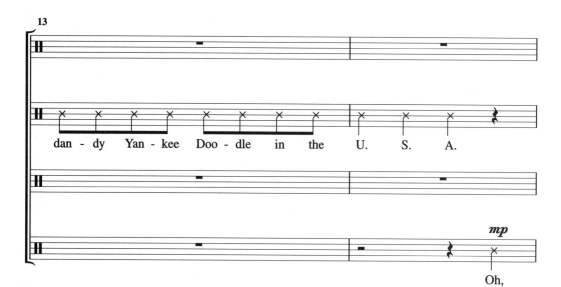

15

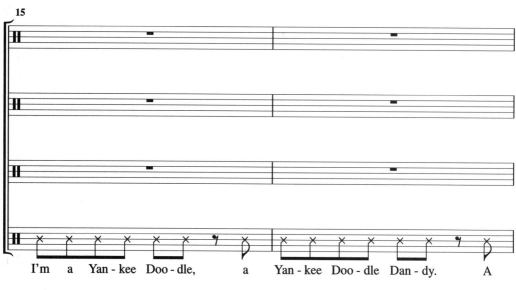

23
Keep it fly - ing high.
Keep it fly - ing high.
Lift that flag.
Lift that flag.
25
cresc.
f
Let it be the sym - bol of Free - dom's cry! Oh,
cresc.
f
Let it be the sym - bol of Free - dom's cry! Oh,
cresc.
f
Let it be the sym - bol of Free - dom's cry! Oh,
cresc.
f
Let it be the sym - bol of Free - dom's cry! Oh,
27
sub. mp
I'm a Yan - kee Doo - dle, a Yan - kee Doo - dle Dan - dy. A

29
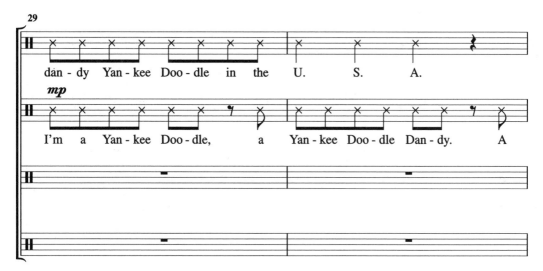

dan - dy Yan - kee Doo - dle in the U. S. A.

mp

I'm a Yan - kee Doo - dle, a Yan - kee Doo - dle Dan - dy. A

31 *build, as if chanting*
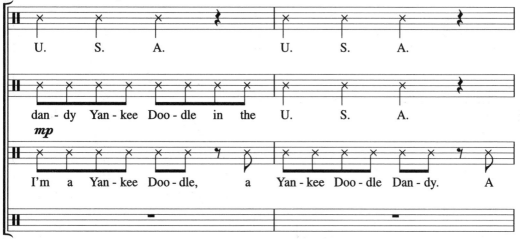

U. S. A. U. S. A.

dan - dy Yan - kee Doo - dle in the U. S. A.

mp

I'm a Yan - kee Doo - dle, a Yan - kee Doo - dle Dan - dy. A

33
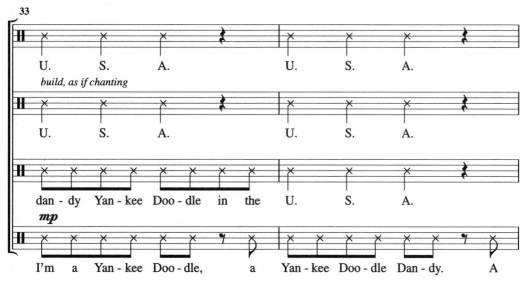

U. S. A. U. S. A.

build, as if chanting

U. S. A. U. S. A.

dan - dy Yan - kee Doo - dle in the U. S. A.

mp

I'm a Yan - kee Doo - dle, a Yan - kee Doo - dle Dan - dy. A

34

GA0112

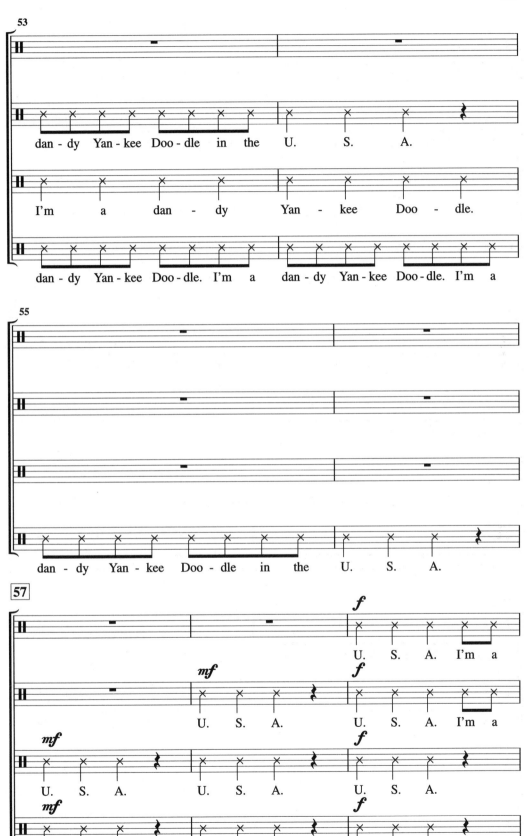

SSHH

for 4-part speech choir, any combination, and drums*

by
GREG GILPIN (ASCAP)

Performance Time: approx. 2:27
Drum part is on page 87.
*Available: Studio Trax CD (CD0349).

GA0112

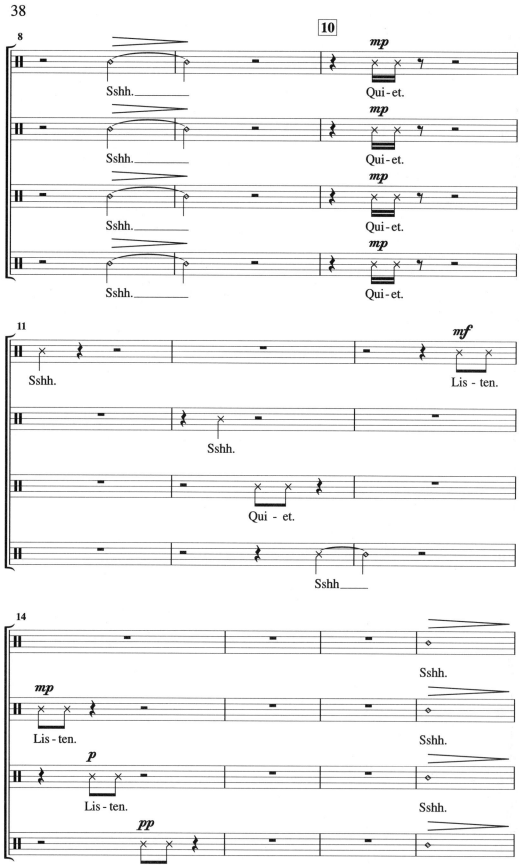

39

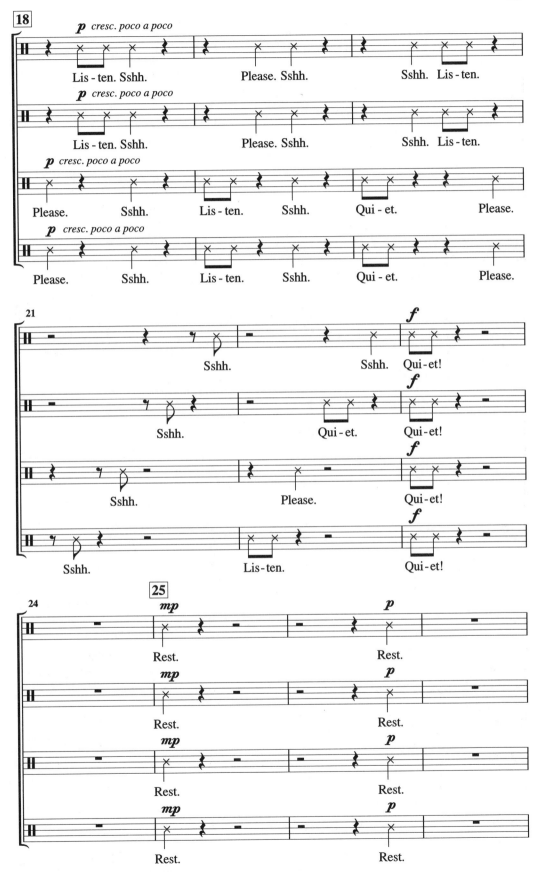

GA0112

40

GA0112

RHYTHM AND DANCE

for 4-part speech choir, any combination, and drums*

by
GREG GILPIN (ASCAP)

Performance Time: approx. 1:54
Drum part is on page 88.
*Available: Studio Trax CD (CD0349).

GA0112

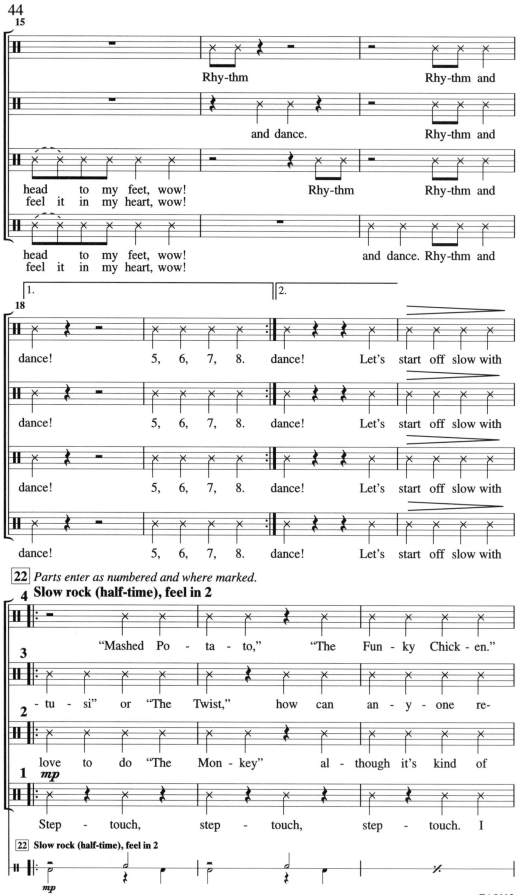

22 *Parts enter as numbered and where marked.*

Slow rock (half-time), feel in 2

Lyrics:
Rhy-thm / Rhy-thm and
and dance. / Rhy-thm and
head to my feet, wow! / feel it in my heart, wow! / Rhy-thm / Rhy-thm and
head to my feet, wow! / feel it in my heart, wow! / and dance. Rhy-thm and

dance! / 5, 6, 7, 8. / dance! Let's start off slow with
dance! / 5, 6, 7, 8. / dance! Let's start off slow with
dance! / 5, 6, 7, 8. / dance! Let's start off slow with
dance! / 5, 6, 7, 8. / dance! Let's start off slow with

"Mashed Po - ta - to," "The Fun - ky Chick - en."
-tu - si" or "The Twist," how can an - y - one re-
love to do "The Mon - key" al - though it's kind of
Step - touch, step - touch, step - touch. I

22 Slow rock (half-time), feel in 2

GA0112

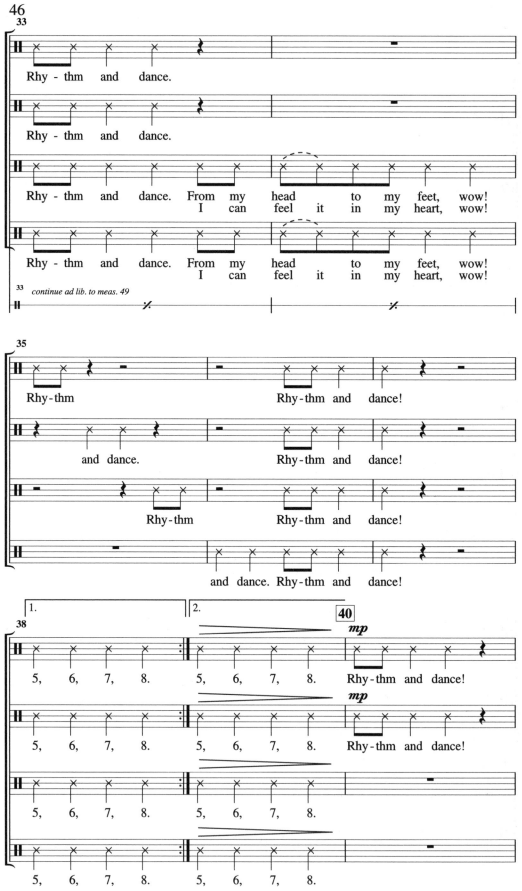

YULETIDE RHYTHM

for 4-part speech choir, any combination, and drums*

by
GREG GILPIN (ASCAP)

Performance Time: approx. 1:52
Drum part is on page 89.
*Available: StudioTrax CD (CD0349)

GA0112

50

GA0112

52

GA0112

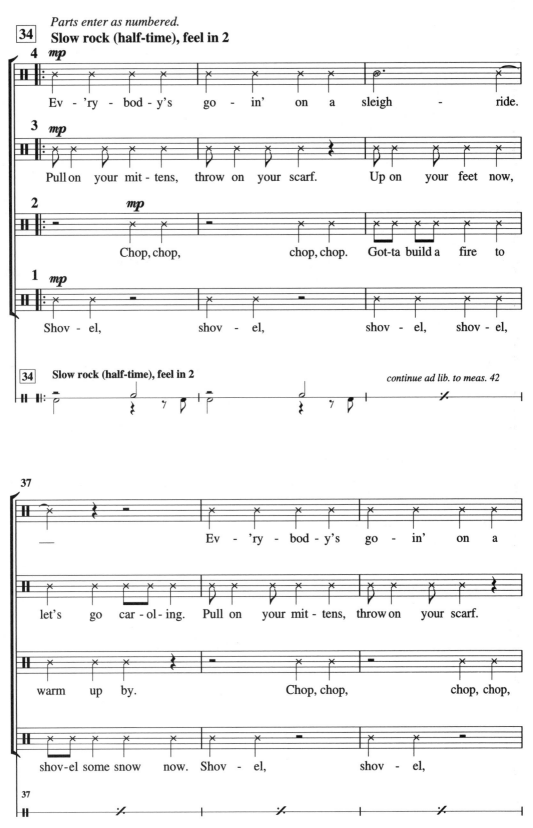

54

42 Tempo I

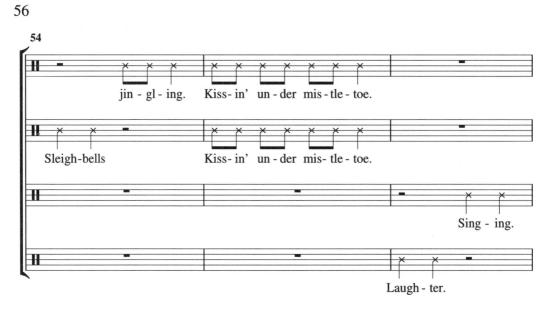

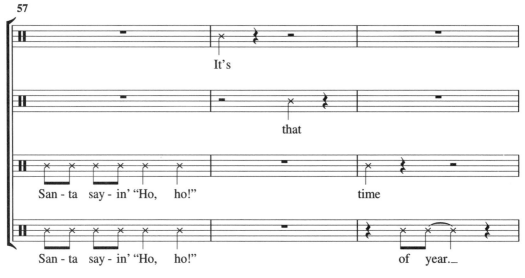

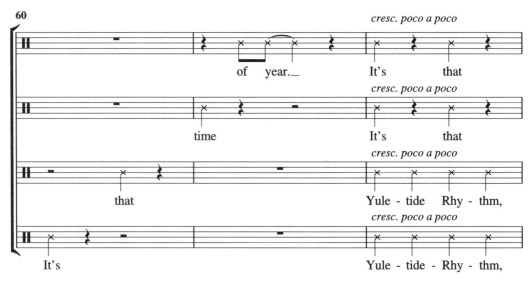

BIG BAND RHYTHM

for 4-part speech choir, any combination, and drums*

by
GREG GILPIN (ASCAP)

Performance Time: approx. 1:56
Drum part is on page 90.
*Available: Studio Trax CD (CD0349).

GA0112

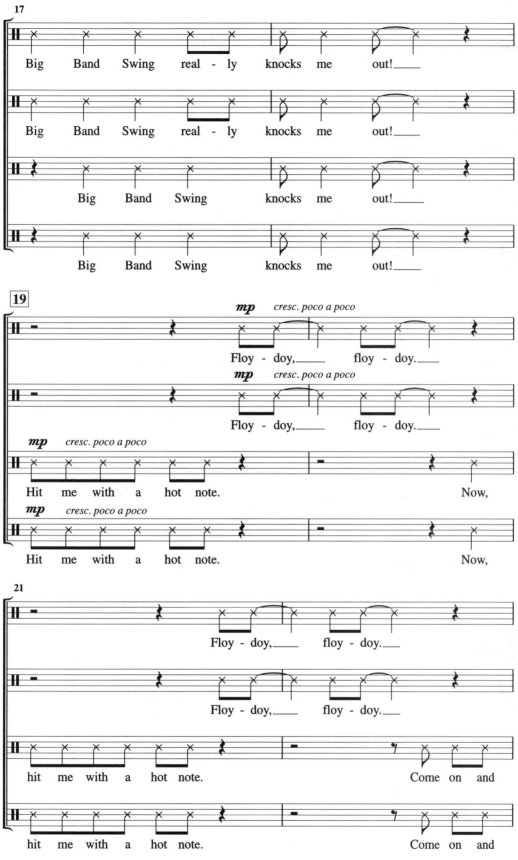

68

GA0112

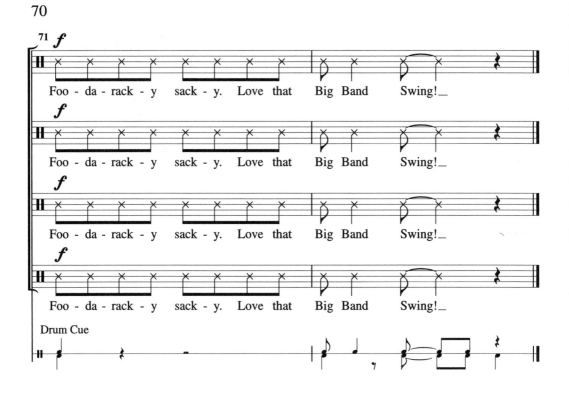

LIFE IS FULL OF RHYTHM

for 4-part speech choir, any combination, and drums*

by
GREG GILPIN (ASCAP)

Performance Time: approx. 1:54
Drum part is on page 91.
*Available: Studio Trax CD (CD0349).

GA0112

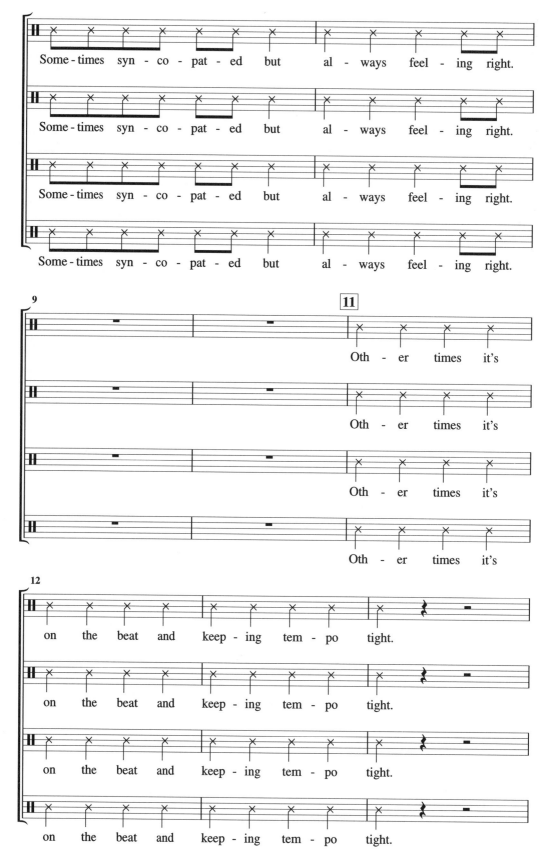

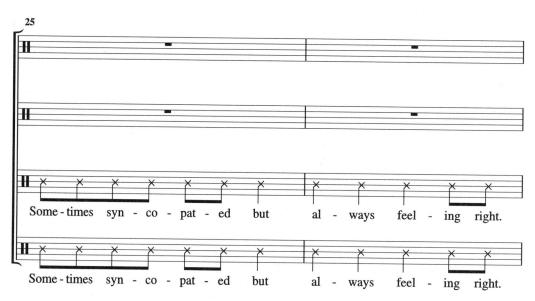

76

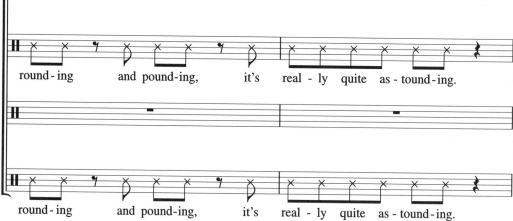

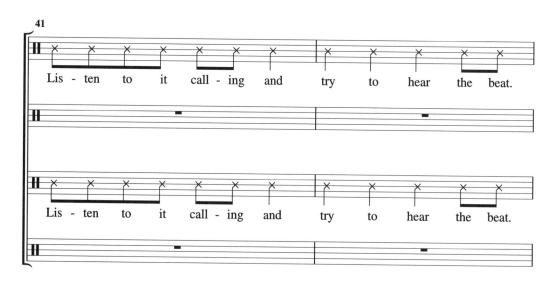

GA0112

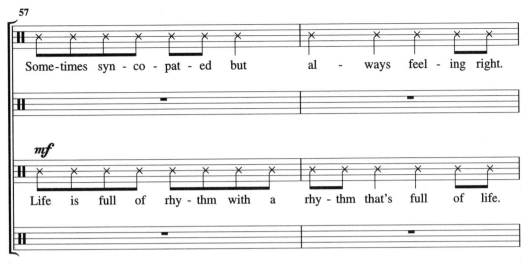

57

Some-times syn - co - pat - ed but   al — ways feel - ing right.

mf

Life is full of rhy - thm with a   rhy - thm that's full of life.

59

Some-times syn - co - pat - ed but   al — ways feel - ing right.

mf

Life is full of rhy - thm with a   rhy - thm that's full of life.

61

Oth — er   times   it's   on   the beat and

Some - times syn - co - pat - ed but   al - ways feel - ing right.

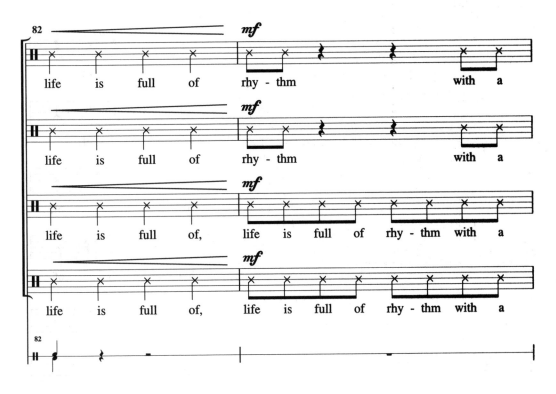

DO YOU FEEL THE RHYTHM?

DRUMS

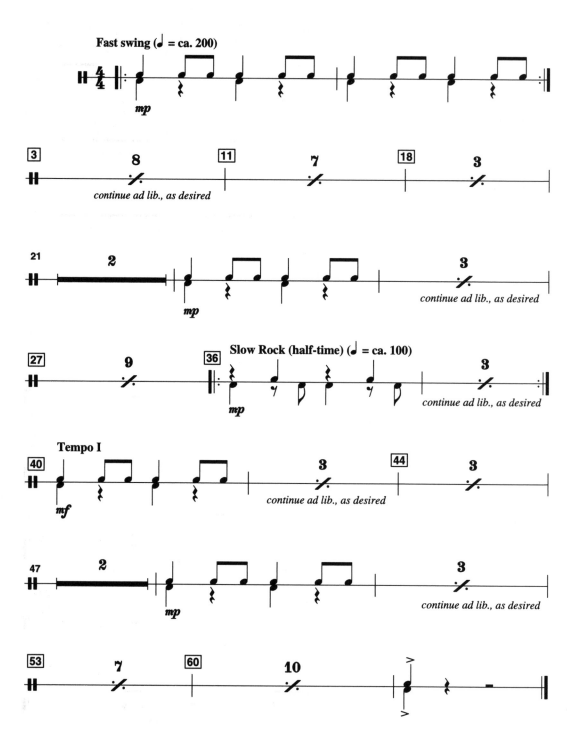

ROCK, RHYTHM AND ROLL

DRUMS

by
GREG GILPIN (ASCAP)

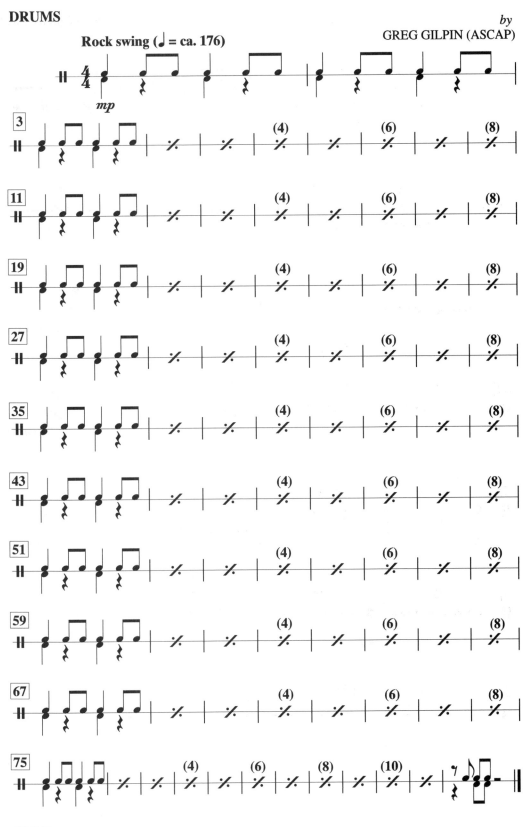

YANKEE DOODLE RHYTHM

DRUMS

by
GREG GILPIN (ASCAP)

GA0112

SSHH

DRUMS

by
GREG GILPIN (ASCAP)

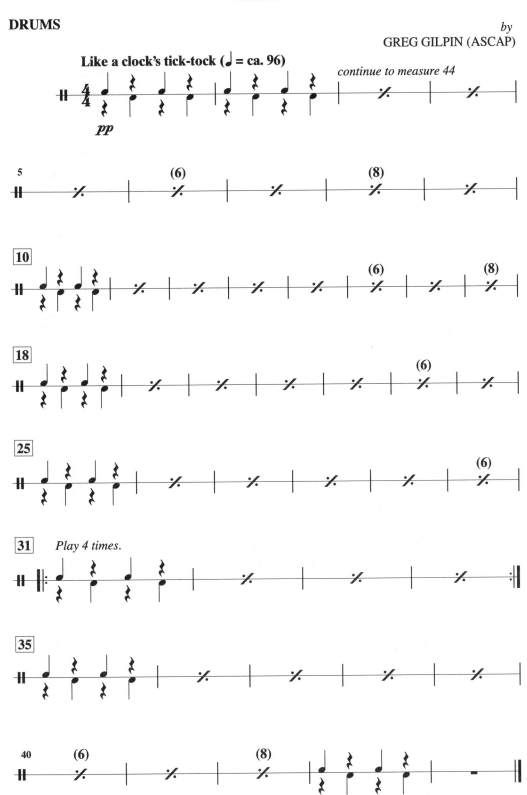

RHYTHM AND DANCE

DRUMS

by
GREG GILPIN (ASCAP)

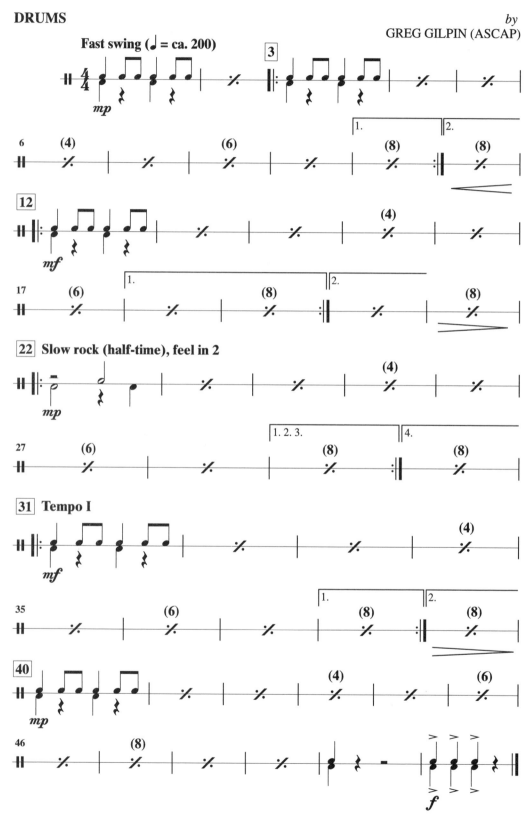

YULETIDE RHYTHM

DRUMS

by
GREG GILPIN (ASCAP)

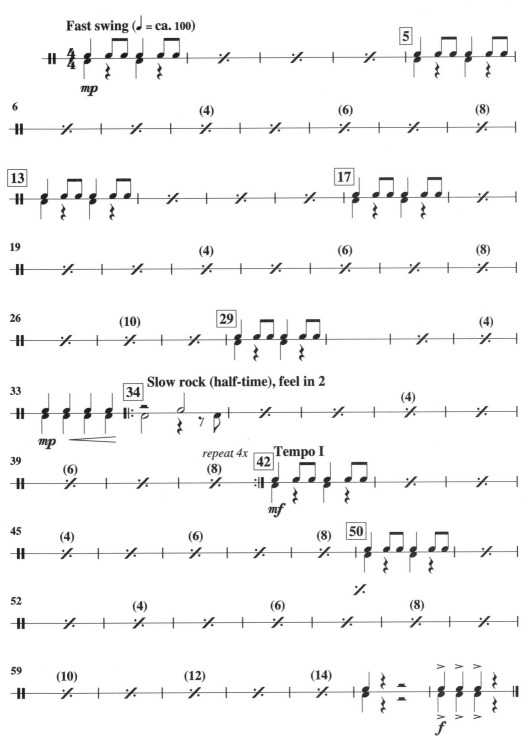

GA0112

BIG BAND RHYTHM

DRUMS

by
GREG GILPIN (ASCAP)

GA0112

LIFE IS FULL OF RHYTHM

DRUMS

by
GREG GILPIN (ASCAP)

Originally from the "Show-Me" state of Missouri, Greg resides in Indianapolis, IN. He is a graduate of Northwest Missouri State University with a Bachelor's Degree in Vocal Music Education, K-12.

Greg is a well-known choral composer and arranger with hundreds of publications to his credit. He does numerous commissions throughout the year and special arranging projects for recorded works. Greg's choral compositions are widely performed and his work "Sleep, My Pretty One" was recently performed throughout the world by the Vienna Boys Choir. He is also in demand as a conductor for choral festivals, all-district and all-state choirs. Greg attends many music educator conventions throughout the year presenting clinics on subjects ranging from movement and choreography to classical literature and sacred music.

He is currently Director of Educational Choral Music for Shawnee Press, Inc. At home in Indianapolis, Greg is busy as a studio musician and producer in the recording industry. These projects include commercial jingles, CD projects, Broadway and Disney. He works or has worked musically with Ray Boltz, Bill and Gloria Gaither, Sandi Patty, David Clydesdale as well as principle pops conductor, Jack Everly and the Indianapolis Symphony Orchestra.

Most recently, Greg can be heard singing background vocals on the Sandi Patty recording "Yuletide Joy" and on the Johnny Mathis holiday CD release "The Christmas Album."